30 Ways To Lift Your Spirits, Not Your *Eyebrows*

SHERNA SPENCER

Book Series: Living Lively

An imprint of **SGS Publishing**
www.LookItsTheBook.com

30 Ways to Lift Your Spirits, not your Eyebrows
Copyright © 2020, by Sherna G. Spencer. All rights reserved. Except as permitted under the U.S. Copyright Act of 1976, no part of this publication may be reproduced, distributed, or transmitted in any form or by any means, or stored in a database or retrieval system, without the prior written permission of the publisher.

Published by JALOUSIE
An imprint of SGS Publishing, LLC
4500 W. Oakland Park Boulevard, Ste 103
Fort Lauderdale, FL 33313

30 Ways to Lift Your Spirits, not your Eyebrows is a work of fiction. Names, characters, places, and incidents are the product of the author's imagination or are used fictionally. Any resemblance to actual events, locales, or persons, living or dead, is coincidental.

Publisher's Cataloging-in-Publication data
Spencer, Sherna G
    30 Ways to Lift Your Spirits, not your Eyebrows
    p.cm
    ISBN 978-0-9787613-6-3
1. Motivational & Inspirational 2. Personal Growth-Happiness 2. Inspirational-Women.
4.Title-

Library of Congress Control number LCN: 2017910889

First Edition: April, 2020
SCANNABLE

Printed in the United States of America

Quantity Discounts are available. Contact the publisher
        www.lookitsthebook.com
        talk@lookitsthebook.com
        954-714-8123

Cover Art: Section of painting by Andy Ballentine

Included Poems

Living Lively 11
Feel Me 22
Seeds for Planting 45
It Will Find You 55
Rise to the Beat 63
Leaving Time 68
The "Why"s Have It 76
Today is Different 79
Here to There 87

Try one, won't you?

It's your *first step* to
Living lively

Lift your **hands** up as **HIGH** as you can and ***say*** as **loudly** as you can: I'm **awake,** let's celebrate!

There are times when we are so caught up with the day-to-day concerns of life, that we forget to *live* in the moment, we forget to take stock of our gifts and talents and recognize just how much we are BLESSED.

You just read this.

Living Lively

Living is what
you do
instinctively
thought
propelled
by action
to satisfy
an innate
need

Living lively
is purposefully
doing something
or some things
that leave
your footprint
that stamps
your mark
on the world

Do it today
the universe
is waiting

There is a special spot
reserved
for you

Lively Living is taking action, recognizing that each moment of your life is precious and making sure that you are sharing yourself, your experiences and your talents with others. In so doing, you are celebrating being on this earth, celebrating living in the moment, celebrating your life.

Sometimes as you are doing this *lively living* you will be laughing, sometimes smiling or crying; but all the while you will be feeling whatever is happening at that time; acknowledge the amazing gift you have been given: the gift of life and the ability to choose.

Another thing that happens when you are doing *lively living* is that your brain and your body are working together harmoniously. They are like an orchestra of experienced musicians, each putting their best effort into playing their instrument.

Think about it this way. Your brain is your body's engine. It conducts and instructs your body, its orchestra. Your senses are the instruments in the orchestra that control your emotions and your spirits. With them, you experience life's highs and lows and the in-betweens; those every day notes that define your life.

You can achieve *lively living* by tuning up your instruments (your senses) and improving your output or impact (create the liveliness in your life). You tune up by changing the experiences you take in. This can be done by changing what you see, touch, or taste, who you interact with and how you interact with them.

You can also make a change with your **SOUND**. Play with how you communicate with the world around you; raise or lower your voice, cry, laugh, sing or hum.

musicians=notes=instruments=orchestra

senses=emotions=body=brain

One other way to make a change is to move your **body**, even if it is only a few steps; or across the city or country, maybe move across the world?

ALL of these actions will create an emotional and physical reaction in you. You will feel it physically and also notice a change in your outlook about life and how you are living it.

Feel Me

Washing the dog outside, she shakes and I am caught and bathed in a rain of soapy water

~

Running, pushing at a good clip, a 5-pound trinket dog chases my sneakers, yapping a noisy blend of fear and bravado. I slow down as I am about to go around the corner and bark back, "Go home!" But both of us stop abruptly, all confidence frozen to silence, as a neighbor being walked by her greyhound meets us. We give them passage and then continue our fiery interaction

~

Pegging an orange with my fingers, the juice sprays up and hits my lip. I lick it off and continue ripping off the rest of the skin, bit by bit, tasting each piece that is revealed

~

The fish propelled his body high, using the pole as its swing. Both hands held the pole firmly, until everything settled down. In a few minutes, the sun burst out, pushing aside the window of thick grey clouds, announcing with its bright, beaming, round face, "I'm awake, let's celebrate!"

You can always practice *lively living*—put it on your schedule every day.

* * * * * *

This book is just the starting point, touching on thirty things you can do, guiding you on **how you can tune your instruments** *(your five senses)* and help you to do more lively living.

* * * * * *

Keep in mind that this tuning may take a bit of effort because you have to push yourself, perhaps out of your comfort zone or beyond what you can do or how far you think you can go to achieve *living lively*.

This **tuning** will require you to change the way you are doing something or some things today.

I remember reading a story about why runners now run faster than they did fifty years ago. The article said that before 1954, the prevailing understanding was that the human body could not withstand running a mile in under four minutes. It was thought that running above such a speed would be dangerous to our health.

According to article, that all changed in 1954, at the Olympics. There, British physician and athlete, Sir Roger Bannister, debunked that myth when he ran the mile in under four minutes.

When asked how he was able to overcome this massive hurdle, he said he did two things: relentlessly trained his mind by visualizing the outcome and second, vigilantly trained his body.

Since that time, it is common to hear of professional athletes and others accomplishing that goal.

Think for a few minutes.

Does that remind you of something,

something that you have done that you worked extremely hard to accomplish?

It was something you were not sure you could do,

but you decided to do it anyway.

Did you have to become extremely focused and even give up something to put in your best effort to achieve that goal?

Take a few more minutes to let that thought sink in.

Do you remember how you felt when you were successful?

Did you feel energized, happy, dare I say that you felt so ecstatic to the point where you wanted to shout, to share your success with the world?

This is how athletes say they feel when they are at their peak of performance—invincible.

Hold that memory close to you and pass it on. While doing so, pass it on with the lessons you learned from that experience to someone who needs some inspiration today.

Practice lively living by pushing beyond the accepted norms.

Practice by **trying something else, something different**.

The best moments in our lives are when we are experiencing life, **doing things** that bring us joy and contentment.

The second best moments in our lives are when we are doing, giving of ourselves to those in need.

This is tuning up, pushing your instruments to the limit, this is doing *lively living*.

Your spirits will be lifted and you will feel more **optimistic**! This will create a difference in your life and health.

Are you ready for your tune-up?

tune your instruments=lift your spirits
=live lively=live longer

live longer=live lively=lift your spirits
=tune your instruments

Start tuning up with one of these

(start small or go radical)

Change NOW. Do It Today.

1. Smile at the next person you see - with your lips AND eyes. Look into their eyes and greet the human, recognize the other person as an emotional being that too, is you. That person is part of you, part of the larger orchestra, the earth's orchestra that we all share.

2. Call someone with whom you really enjoy having a conversation. Live in that moment, extend and enjoy the conversation. I recall hearing about the joy shared by two elderly sports enthusiasts who can no longer travel to the game or to meet each other. They still enjoy sports together, "watching" their favorite teams "together" by phone—imagine their voices shouting above the commentator!

3. Start a twice a year neighborhood meet-up. Bring chairs and food outside and meet and greet your neighbors. Change "I don't even know them… I just run into them when I open the door or take out the trash or as they drive in or out or walk to the elevator," to "Shannon lives over there or Jack and Jody live next door."

4. Write out two or three things you would ideally like to be doing on a Saturday or a Sunday afternoon—take a picture of it and put it somewhere you can see it every day. Write down the name of someone (or a few people) who you think can help you to make that ideal a reality.

Go and ask for company or help! Keep asking until you find the right person or persons. Thomas Edison is reported to have tried over 10,000 times to make and perfect the light bulb!

5. Taste extremes. Taste something sweet and then something sour, something hot and then something cold, something peppery and then something bland.

Your senses and taste buds (in fact your entire body), reacts when it hits your tongue doesn't it? Pause and let it idle and live in that moment, feeling those new sensations. Now taste something that you really love.

6. Write down three to five songs or musical compositions you would like to hear right now. Find and play them or go and experience them where they are being performed.

Invite someone to join you.

7. Play a game with a child. You might find as I did, that laughter or maybe a few tears will emerge as winnings and losses pile up. My daughter, an unhappy loser, once said, "you bested me, this is a stupid game!"

Seeds for Planting

Your deeds send
seeds or weeds
into the stratosphere

An angel
tabulates them
and returns the list to you
for confirmation

When the time comes
for your review
you rail
you twitch
seeing
a life tied together
with weeds

Spill buckets of seeds
across the billowy clouds
They will return to you
as raindrops
dancing to the ground
on a light breeze
welcomed
ready for planting
anew

8. Make a meal from a recipe book or create your own concoction.

Make something or some things that you can share with someone or a few persons. Create or do something to leave behind a memory of you!

Start it. Write a poem or song, make a hat or dress. Record your voice. Embellish something that is already made or fix something that needs your expertise (help to paint that wall or read that essay).

Lift some weights or read out loud for yourself or for others. That's your brain and body working in wonderful tandem.

You were intentionally designed.

You are special.

9. Re-gift something you have not used for a while. Send it to a friend or acquaintance and pin or tape a note on it, telling the receiver of your desire that they enjoy and treasure it. You can also donate it to a nonprofit organization.

10. Start writing a **thank-you note** or a letter every week. You could deliver it personally, send it through regular mail or send it express, for no particular reason, other than to acknowledge and express your gratitude—sometimes in a big way.

If the receiver is close to you, put it somewhere where they are likely to discover it. The love is coming back to you or to your loved ones—trust in this truth.

11. Flip the switch on your body—if you like a hot environment, spend some time in a very cool place or vice versa. Your body speaks to you through your skin, nostrils, head, fingers and feet.

Listen to it.

12. If you are a loud talker, be silent or speak softly for a while. Try this. Taste your words, let them slowly, softly, drift out. If you are usually soft spoken, raise your voice a few octaves.

Pay attention to how your senses react. How does your body feel? What do you feel like doing in that moment? Go with the flow.

13. Your orchestra lives and breathes through the efforts of the human touch. Sit next to someone; put your body next to theirs. Don't observe any personal space, so you can exchange the warmth, the energy and life force that make us human.

Each of us has space or zone around ourselves that we consider our "personal space," where we feel that others should not intrude without permission. When you are in that space you can see and feel the person breathe or their heart beating.

Think again about and appreciate how your marvelously designed body takes you through the day, alerting you and guiding you about your environment (did I just hear the child cry, footsteps, there is a stone I need to walk around, it's windy, I will need to bring a jacket, I smell my favorite dish being cooked) and about the people you meet (that person looks sad, skeptical, happy, angry, worried).

Our orchestra is always at work. From the moment we awaken, its instruments are ready to take us through the day.

14. Teach someone whatever you love to do. While you are taking your time to transfer your knowledge, you are fine tuning your instruments—isn't that a great trade off!

Watch your student's eyes come alive when they fully grasp the information and excel—through your guidance! That is your footprint. It will outlive you. Let them say "I am excellent at such or such, "your name here" taught me well."

It Will Find You

We all want to know
that there is a reason for our being
We search our minds
at times
in quiet solitude

We rise each day
hoping that
as certain as the dawn
we will discover our purpose

It is written
that all men are created equal
on purpose.

Keep looking
it will find you

15. Have a one-on-one with the earth's elements; press the soles of your feet into the ground or the grass or the dirt. If you are at the beach, push your feet deep in the sand until you feel the coolness surround your ankles. Feel the earth's essence taking you to a serene place.

If you are inside, put your bare feet on the cool tile or in warm water in a basin or in the tub. Close your eyes and inhale and feel its calming energy flow through your body.

There is a **reason** why **you are here** on this earth at this time. You are NOT supposed to *just* **breathe** and silently **purr** your way from womb to tomb. You are **supposed to be** doing lively Living.

16. As you go about your day, hum your favorite song. Liven your day by remembering the words or the melody and the memories the song evokes.

You can take it up a notch. Do an all-out Sing Out Loud. Your body will love it—someone might see you and ask why you seem content, tell them that you are doing *Lively Living*.

17. Close your eyes and say to yourself, "I have done well." Say, "I have done the best that I can." If you mean it, you have. Allow that feeling of accomplishment and satisfaction to flow through your mind and body. Share that thought with someone, they may need to hear it to help them to *push* **a little harder**.

If you can't find that truth inside yourself right now, renew your efforts and find a helper—your orchestra sometimes needs another instrument to make it rock.

18. Every day your nose is bombarded with scents. Move away from overly pungent odors. Get some fresh air ... take deep breaths. Breathe in from the diaphragm—the deep part of your chest, slowly pull it up. Release it just as slowly through your mouth. Close your eyes and do it again three times.

19. Try rearranging your cells' (not your phone's) expectations. You could play by skipping rope alone or ask the next-door neighbors to join you in the double dutch—maybe hopscotch. Walk a few extra steps; run; ride a horse, dance, throw a ball or balance the hoola-hoop on your hips for a few minutes—it's not as easy as you think!

Push through, enjoy the result.
Orchestra tuning can take time.

Rise to the Beat

Rise to the beat
the song stirs within you

take the hand of the little ones
connect their minds, hearts souls and bodies
to be one

Rise to the beat
the ancestors reach
to anoint you
to appoint you
as transmitter
as teacher

Rise to the beat
one by one
one on one
take it now
pass it on

Feel the drumbeat

20. Think of a lone seal standing on the ice, surveying its territory.

Envision the sun streaming in, cascading from the sky, exposing the Arctic's stark black and white terrain. It is still, there is nothing to do except to BE.

See her.

See that beautiful seal, tall and majestic, in its surroundings. Picture yourself there with her, inhaling the crisp, cold air. Be her.

Breathe.

21. Welcome a newcomer. Make a rule if you see someone in a new terrain standing alone, go over and greet them. Treat them as you would if they were a guest in your home. Be their guide in their new arena, they will really appreciate your consideration— you might find a lifelong friend or someone who can open the door to something for you or you might be the door opener. It is said that we do not know if someone new comes into our life for a particular reason, a season or a lifetime- only time will tell.

22. Find a picture that you love, one that brightens your mood just by looking at it. Blow it up so it is LARGE.

Hang it in a prominent place in your home or personal space where you work.

Leaving Time

What do you take from a smile
an exchange of thoughts that lingers
long after the words are spoken
"We could get married and run away to Ecuador"

The earth stopped
then started again
It released a strong wind
that made music
it danced
and whistled its way through the thin, wispy grass
straight out to the shore
where it whipped the waters high
then smashed down
shivering
burrowing
into the deep
reaching the frontier
between
heaven
and earth
.
Ecuador
"What's in Ecuador?"

23. Decide to be a big brother, sister, uncle or aunt for a child in need. Tomorrow, they may take your hand and be your guide. Nurture them, talk to them, be their sound box, supporter and cheerleader. Watch them excel and make you proud.

24. Don't give up all of your wall space to display the creations of others. Create a celebration wall in your home. Take your trophies, certificates, drawings or whatever you are proud of—you have them in a box or drawer! Put them there on your celebration wall, so you can see them every day and relive your accomplishments or those of your loved ones.

25. Take a phrase or sentence from a piece of writing that touches you in some way. Write it down three times. As you write, open your imagination and experience the words. Re-read it often. Put it in your purse or wallet next to your identification or credit card so you will see it each time you go into your purse or wallet. Change it ever so often, Keep them and put them in a frame for your wall.

26. Find an opportunity to do something good for someone before the end of the day today. Keep your ears and eyes attuned as you go about your day. You will hear about something that needs YOUR unique touch and attention.

27. Sit under a tree and imagine the history it has seen and the number of people it has sheltered. If it is a fruit tree, think of the number of people it has fed. In a whisper, ask it how it does its job and listen. It has a purpose, just like you.

28. Keep learning through reading. Read an article today. Read at least four new books every year (take it up to 8 next year). Read at least one book from an international author.

29. Write it out and take back your life. Write a letter and name the perpetrator of any pain, anger, hurt, embarrassment or loss you have felt. Take as many sessions as you need, to write it all out. Just keep going until your senses tell you everything has been purged. At the end, you might feel drained.

Take a long nap.

Do it.

After you have rested, wake up and set a new goal for your life. Get yourself ready to play a new song, announcing the new YOU.

The "Why"s Have It

Q: Why do I have to…?
A: Getting from here to there
means
moving
leaving behind a comfortable
existence

~

Q: Why did I do…?
A: The only way to know if you made the right decision
is to reflect

Reflect upon what you learned

Learning
means finding the truth
behind your actions
The action means more than the words

~

Q: Why am I here…?
A: Justify your existence

Make the world remember
your face
Leave a trace
some place

30. Have you ever heard a rooster crow? He does it every morning of his life. There is something in his DNA that tells him to speak out every morning. He doesn't know why or even that his crow is his talent. His voice told us before clocks, telling us that it was time to rise and start our day.

Speak. It's one of your talents, use your voice for good today.

Make today different!

Today is Different

What a difference a day makes
Today
Not yesterday
Not the day before yesterday
Not last Monday
Not two weeks ago
Not last year
Not your last birthday
Not your last anniversary
Not the last time you thought to do
whatever you did not do

What a difference a day makes
Today
it's 24 hours
6 are gone before you awaken
cherish the second thought that reminds you
of something you almost forgot
cherish that instinct
it guides you
cherish the way you talk
cherish the way you smile
cherish the way you walk
cherish the way you feel
as you slide yourself into your clothes

like the hug of a
button down shirt

What a difference a day makes
Today
Hold the strands of the air around you
organize them
whispers of love and motivation
here
whispers of negativity
there
behind me

Move with a purpose
eyes wide open
striding
gliding
towards the stars
where your future lies

Today is the day to cherish

There is something you have wanted to do. You have been thinking about it (and thinking of all the reasons why you cannot start it). <u>Write it down</u> – make a list of the steps (you can go back and perfect this later). **Just start**; make a call, go to the store, go on line, go to your garage, go into the backyard, press the "on" button. **Start it** as you are reading this, don't let the opportunity for self-fulfillment pass you by. **Seize** this moment as yours. We are only sure of this moment in time, what happens next is anyone's guess. You are in the here and now. What are you doing to make this your moment?

Cherish *life*

You're reading this while someone is not able to do so.

You took this book in your hands and held it and someone cannot do that.

You are seeing the colors, feeling the texture and now you are raising your eyebrows as you think

"Where is this going"

Here is the point. You moved, read, felt and thought instinctively.

We do that all day long, **living our lives unconsciously** until something happens that forces us to stop and realize that living is a precious gift.

Be conscious of this gift. You are here to be something, to be a part of this cosmos at this time **on purpose**. Do something or some things every day to make your mark on this earth at this time. It will make you feel more lively and happy. This is *lively living*.

Do something or some things every day. Start by celebrating when you wake up.

The new day is a new opportunity to leave your footprint on the world.

Celebrate the moment you awake.

Here to There

One moment you are here
the next, you are there.
Unfortunately you can't choose to remain here
or not to move to there.

You are
then
you were.
There is no standing still.

It is your decision what you do
when you are
here or there.
You decide.

At any moment in time
you can say "I am here doing " X or Y, but
in the next moment
you will need to say "I was there and did Z."

Life is best lived in the moment
when you are here, aware,
in the know
in the now.

There you have it... ***30 Ways to Lift Your Spirits***

Slowly reread pages 31 and 76.

Which are you going to do today?

Write it down.

_____
_____
_____

Now go out there and *live lively*.

Use the next 20 pages to send a quick or long note to a few people who have touched your life or whose lives you want to touch. Write it. Rip it out. Put it in an envelope. Snail mail it. You can make a difference in someone's life. You will feel good and so will they.

Leave a trace, some place...

Let us know their reaction. Send us a note to:
talk@lookitsthebook.com

30 Ways To Lift Your Spirits, Not Your Eyebrows

SHERNA SPENCER

30 Ways To Lift Your Spirits, Not Your Eyebrows

S H E R N A   S P E N C E R

30 Ways To Lift Your Spirits, Not Your *Eyebrows*

SHERNA   SPENCER

30 Ways To Lift Your Spirits, Not Your *Eyebrows*

S   H   E   R   N   A   S   P   E   N   C   E   R

30 Ways To Lift Your Spirits, Not Your *Eyebrows*

SHERNA SPENCER

30 Ways To Lift Your Spirits, Not Your Eyebrows

SHERNA SPENCER

30 Ways To Lift Your Spirits, Not Your Eyebrows

SHERNA SPENCER

30 Ways To Lift Your Spirits, Not Your *Eyebrows*

SHERNA SPENCER

30 Ways To Lift Your Spirits, Not Your *Eyebrows*

SHERNA SPENCER

30 Ways To Lift Your Spirits, Not Your *Eyebrows*

SHERNA SPENCER

30 Ways To Lift Your Spirits, Not Your *Eyebrows*

S H E R N A   S P E N C E R

30 Ways To Lift Your Spirits, Not Your Eyebrows

SHERNA   SPENCER

30 Ways To Lift Your Spirits, Not Your *Eyebrows*

S   H   E   R   N   A   S   P   E   N   C   E   R

30 Ways To Lift Your Spirits, Not Your *Eyebrows*

SHERNA SPENCER

30 Ways To Lift Your Spirits, Not Your *Eyebrows*

S H E R N A   S P E N C E R

30 Ways To Lift Your Spirits, Not Your *Eyebrows*

S H E R N A   S P E N C E R

30 Ways To Lift Your Spirits, Not Your Eyebrows

SHERNA SPENCER

30 Ways To Lift Your Spirits, Not Your *Eyebrows*

SHERNA   SPENCER

30 Ways To Lift Your Spirits, Not Your *Eyebrows*

S   H   E   R   N   A   S   P   E   N   C   E   R

30 Ways To Lift Your Spirits, Not Your *Eyebrows*

S   H   E   R   N   A   S   P   E   N   C   E   R

About the Author

Sherna Spencer's roots spring from the Island of Jamaica. Her love of books and language began there in a Parish library in Manchester. After moving to the U.S, she attended Le Moyne College in upstate New York. There, she obtained a Bachelors degree, with dual majors in English and Spanish. She continued her studies in Italy and thereafter completed her law degree at the University of Miami School of Law. She is currently an attorney in Fort Lauderdale, Florida where she was the host of a radio program about immigration and nationality law, for 9 years.

Other Books By The Author

Musing Aloud, Allowed
Three Echoes Dancing
It's the Context
Whether Your Storm

www.ingramcontent.com/pod-product-compliance
Lightning Source LLC
Chambersburg PA
CBHW080520300426
44112CB00018B/2803